KV-340-422

CONTENTS

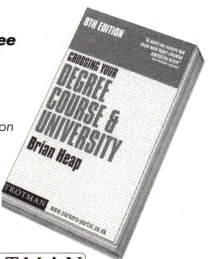

GETTING INTO

Getting into Hotels and Catering
Second edition

This second edition published in 2002
by Trotman and Company Ltd
2 The Green, Richmond, Surrey TW9 1PL

© Trotman and Company Limited 2002

British Library Cataloguing in Publication Data
A catalogue record for this book is available from the
British Library.

ISBN 0 85660 837 8

Typeset by Mac Style Ltd, Scarborough, N. Yorkshire

Printed and bound in Great Britain
by Bell & Bain Ltd

INTRODUCTION

BACKGROUND

If you decide to make a career in hotels and catering, you will be joining an industry that employs nearly 1.8 million people – and is still expanding. It is expected that by the year 2005 some 170,000 new jobs will have been created. (This is a shortfall on previous predictions which estimated a required workforce of nearly 2.5 million, but nevertheless it is a sizeable increase.)

WHAT ELSE IS SIGNIFICANT?

- There are more opportunities for young people in hotels and catering than in many career areas. Nearly one third of employees are under the age of 24.
- Job opportunities are varied. Places of employment range from five-star hotels to residential care establishments, from pubs to cruise ships, hospitals to fast food restaurants, while individual employers range in size from international hotel groups to family guest houses.

The industry is usually classified into two main sectors: the commercial sector and the hospitality services sector.

The *commercial sector* includes establishments that are run for profit:

- aircraft
- clubs
- cruise ships
- fast food restaurants
- guest houses
- holiday centres
- hotels
- leisure centres
- motorway service areas
- pubs
- restaurants
- trains
- wine bars.

1

It is the larger sector, employing two thirds of the workforce, and is expanding the more rapidly of the two, largely due to an increase in the numbers of fast food restaurants and in pubs serving meals.

The *hospitality services sector* is smaller. If you chose to work here, you would be employed in establishments where providing food and drink is not the primary function. You could, for instance, work in:

- colleges
- companies' staff restaurants
- hospitals
- nursing homes
- prisons

- residential care establishments
- social or sports clubs
- schools
- the school meals service
- universities.

WHAT'S HAPPENING IN HOTELS AND CATERING?

First, the industry had a tough year in 2001. It hadn't recovered from the outbreak of foot and mouth disease in the spring of that year when the tragedy on September 11th dealt it another blow. There was a dramatic decline in tourism on both counts – with 14 per cent fewer visitors to the UK in 2001. Foot and mouth did not just affect hotels and guesthouses in the countryside. When some major sporting events were cancelled, cities were dealt a blow too. There was a drop in the numbers of both business travellers and tourists using airlines all over the world after September 11th. This affected all kinds of tourism establishments – including hotels near airports which were used to receiving both business customers and air crew. (The UK tourism industry as a whole lost £2 billion in 2001.) Sadly, some small businesses didn't survive. The larger employers, however, tightened their belts and waited. They had to halt some expansion programmes. Some had to make staff redundant. They all had to think of ways of attracting customers back. In many cases, this meant reducing prices. Large hotels had to reduce their room rates. And how many 'Two meals for the price of one' or 'Eat at £x before 7pm' offers were around?

Official sources have provided some assistance. In the autumn of 2001 the British Tourist Authority, charged with promoting Britain overseas, mounted a large advertising campaign, hoping to attract overseas visitors back. In spring 2002, the government contributed £19 million to the campaign. This was to enable advertising to be targeted at seven key markets between April and September – Belgium, Canada, France, Germany, Ireland, The Netherlands and the USA. (Sixty per cent of Britain's foreign visitors come from these countries.) Advertising was due to cover the whole of Britain, focusing particularly on 'Royal Heritage' and the attractions of the Queen's Golden Jubilee. It was hoped to attract one million extra visitors during this period.

The prospects for new entrants to hotels and catering establishments, though, did not reduce greatly. Why? Because there was always a staff shortage. Fewer people have always wanted to work in hotels and catering than the industry needed. The Job Centre of just one English historic city, for example, was already carrying over 90 job vacancies on a regular basis when a major chain decided to build a new hotel that would be looking for staff.

NEW OPPORTUNITIES

Nearly 60,000 people work in pubs and bars. The licensed retail trade is a growing area of employment. There are now 120,000 licensed premises across the country. Many of the staff working in them, however, are part time. This means that *managers* have to be well trained and flexible – willing to turn their hand to any job that needs doing, in addition to increasing the pub's profits. There is still a route for working your way up from bar staff to manager, but some of the larger chains are now looking for a number of people with degrees or diplomas (not always in catering) to be future managers.

There are also more opportunities to run your own business. Openings have always existed for tenants or owner managers in the licensed trade or for people to establish and run their own hotels, restaurants or guest houses, if they can raise the capital – no small amount! The average purchase price of a pub is around £275,000, while the initial cost of fixtures, furnishings and stock can range from £10,000 to £100,000. The development of franchising has brought running their own catering business within the reach of more people. (Under a franchise arrangement, people still have to raise a certain sum of money but they use this to rent premises, and a brand name. They buy supplies from the company, prepare standard meals and receive help in advertising and training staff.) Pizza and other fast food restaurants are major opportunity providers.

WORKING CONDITIONS

Working conditions and low pay are responsible for hotel and catering work not being everybody's first choice of career. Is the reputation justified? The industry certainly has a reputation for poor training, but this is not always justified. Large employers usually provide very good training. However, smaller employers – the majority – have not always known how to train properly or what kind of assistance was available. Much is being done to improve this. The smaller employers are, through the introduction of Modern Apprenticeships and similar schemes, being given an opportunity to make improvements in this area. (The Hospitality Training Foundation, which is the National Training Organisation* for the industry, not only specifies the kind of training that must be given – and this includes guaranteed off-the-job training from 2002 – but also recommends levels of pay.) Hours are improving as employers have to compete to retain staff. Split shifts in kitchens, for example, are often unpopular with staff, and a manager who is prepared to do away with these is more likely to keep his or her employees. Some people are very well rewarded; others not. Often people doing the less skilled jobs are paid only the national minimum wage – but in the profit-making sector they can earn tips. Managers *can* earn high salaries and usually receive annual bonuses depending on their profits. Most people get some perks. It is normal to get free meals on duty and some employees are given free uniforms and cheap accommodation.

It is very difficult to quote figures for salaries and benefits since they vary so much from one employer to another. However, as a very general guide, you might expect to earn the following approximate amounts in different jobs.

---

* By the time you read this, many National Training Organisations (NTOs) will have been replaced by Sector Skills Councils.

Chef de partie (Section head)	£11,500 to £16,500
Sous chef	up to £19,000
Head chef	up to £26,000
(Many head chefs earn considerably more)	
Deputy general manager	£14,000 to £20,000
Food service staff	£8,000
Head housekeeper	over £23,000
Head waiter	£14,000
(Head waiters earn more and receive large tips in famous restaurants)	
Hotel general manager	over £30,000
(Some managers and deputies earn much more, especially in large hotels)	
Housekeeper	£15,000 to £18,000
Junior or commis chef	£9,500
Kitchen assistant or porter	£6,000 to £9,000
Porter	£7,000 to £10,000
Receptionist	£12,000
Restaurant or catering manager	£20,000 to over £40,000
Room attendant	£8,000 to £10,000

ENTRY QUALIFICATIONS

One benefit of choosing a career in hotels and catering is that there is room for people with all kinds of educational qualifications – and there are prospects for promotion. It is still possible to enter with modest qualifications and work your way up. Many a housekeeper has started out as a room attendant; many a restaurant manager as a waiter. Supervisory and managerial-level positions are within the reach of people who might not be able to progress to the same extent in other employment areas. It is true to say, however, that many senior managers now have either degree or higher diploma level qualifications behind them.

Two things count more than all the paper qualifications in the world in this industry: personality and experience. No-one can reach a management position without gaining some experience in different areas of the work. No-one who is not interested in customer service and teamwork should enter the industry at all! (Teamwork is essential. One or two people who feature as case studies mention that everyone, even senior managers, pitches in and lends a hand at busy times.)

FACTS AND FIGURES

There are 289,949 businesses in the UK that provide food, beverages and/or accommodation.

Sixty per cent of jobs are in the commercial sector.

Forty per cent are in businesses in which hospitality is not the main purpose – ie schools, hospitals etc.

Forty-five per cent of employees work in large companies.

But over 90 per cent of businesses are small.

The largest increase in new jobs is expected to be in chain pubs, budget hotels and coffee shops.

Chapter 1
PERSONAL QUALITIES

Each individual job has its own requirements – and these are summarised at the end of each job description in Chapter 3. However, there are some skills and personal qualities that are common to most of them. First of all you need to be physically fit (except to do a very small number of backroom jobs such as accounts, switchboard or other administrative work which can be done seated). Most of the other jobs involve a good deal of standing and walking. Some require heavy lifting. A kitchen porter, for instance, unloads delivery lorries and carries large loads in the kitchen. Bar work involves lifting barrels from cellars and unloading supplies from lorries. Room attendants often find the work very tiring at first, until they get up to speed – and even then they are doing physical work all through their shift. Chefs must be able to work in hot conditions. Remember the saying 'If you can't stand the heat, get out of the kitchen'? Managers in this industry also spend a lot of time on their feet. They spend a certain amount of time in meetings, but in the daily course of their jobs they move around the hotel, restaurant, bar, coffee shop or other outlet supervising staff and speaking with guests/clients as they do so.

Willingness to work irregular hours is another 'must'. If you join an industry that provides a 24-hour, seven-day-a-week service, you are bound to be working at times when other people (your guests) are enjoying themselves. You might have to work at weekends and on bank holidays, including Christmas Day. Exceptions to this are some jobs in the catering sector. Catering managers, school meals organisers and their staff can work hours that are more regular and much shorter than elsewhere in the hospitality industry.

You would have to enjoy working with other people. Anyone working in accommodation services or a food and beverage department or outlet needs strong customer care skills – and a smart appearance. They will be meeting customers constantly – and if they don't provide a good and efficient service, the customers will not come back. Managers as well as service staff frequently meet clients, for example to discuss requirements for special events. So a genuine interest in providing a service is important.

Working with people does not always mean with customers. There are no customers in a kitchen but staff work together in close teams and help each other out when necessary. In fact, this happens throughout the hotel and catering industry. People have to be flexible and willing at times to help out in what is not their own job. Housekeepers may have to clean rooms and make beds when they are short-staffed. General managers have been known to roll up their sleeves and cook or take a turn behind the reception desk or even make beds. Teamwork skills are essential.

This is not a career area for clock-watchers or people who see job boundaries as fixed.

Chapter 2
TRAINING

There are several different ways of training for jobs in the hotel and catering industry, ranging from from what is called on-the-job training (ie for people who are in employment and are taught the work by senior staff), to full-time courses in further education or private colleges, right through to degree and postgraduate level. The route you choose will depend on several factors:

- the type of job you wish to train for;
- the opportunities in the area where you live (unless of course you are willing to move away from home);
- the age at which you wish to start training;
- the educational qualifications you have; and
- your own preference where there are several routes to a particular job. (There usually are!)

THE IMPORTANCE OF PRACTICAL TRAINING

Whichever method you choose, there is no substitute for work experience. The skills needed to work in hospitality cannot be learned from books. So, even though there are degree courses in hotel and catering management, students on the courses do not spend all their time in lecture rooms, absorbing theory. The courses have a high practical content and can contain up to as much as one year's placement in the industry so that students can learn at first hand. During such periods, students learn to do all levels of job. Even a highly qualified student hoping eventually to manage a top establishment will have spent time working in the kitchens, portering, etc. There are sound reasons for this. One reason is that managers rarely have to ask a staff member to do jobs that they don't fully understand themselves (and can therefore understand the pressures) and another is that they know exactly which skills they are looking for when they recruit staff.

The different routes will now be explained and you will be able to work out the advantages and/or disadvantages of each one. Don't forget though, that as mentioned in the Introduction, this is an industry in which it is still possible to enter at one level and gain promotion to another. If you then move on to Chapter 3 – Career Paths, you will see brief notes on which entry methods apply to each job.

FULL-TIME EMPLOYMENT

It is possible to make a start in most of the jobs below supervisory level – for example as bar staff, cleaners, trainee chefs/cooks, food service staff, kitchen assistants, porters, receptionists, reservations staff and room attendants – and receive all the necessary training while being paid.

Many well-known names in the industry – particularly on the food preparation side – began as juniors and worked their way up.

What are the benefits of this route?

- You would receive a wage.
- You would be training in a real situation, working with customers, in a kitchen, accommodation area or front office and learning how to cope with problems as they arose. You would experience the pressure of busy times.
- Some employers only use this route. There are some head chefs, for instance, who say that they will only recruit chefs who have trained in a busy kitchen, rather than at a college.

And the drawbacks?

Some people find the pace too fast and would be better suited to a full-time course where they can practise tasks until they are sure that they are confident – and then carry out the tasks face to face with customers.

The job may be known by the title 'junior', 'trainee' or 'apprentice'. The exact title does not matter. What does matter is the quality of experience and training it offers. If you decide to look for a full-time job, you should aim for one with an employer who will give you good training. Many of them either send trainees to attend college courses as part of their training or arrange for them to be assessed in the workplace for the award of National Vocational Qualifications (NVQs) or Scottish Vocational Qualifications (SVQs) to Levels 1 or 2. (For an explanation of these terms, see Chapter 4 – Professional qualifications.)

Work-based training programmes

Some employers prefer to train their junior staff through one of the government training programmes. These schemes are not only for people who are unable to obtain full-time employment.

Programmes come under various names, but what they have in common is an approved level of training to agreed national standards which is followed by all trainees at their places of work and leads to the award of an NVQ or SVQ. In addition, they get some off-the-job training – which may mean attending a college – to obtain a technical certificate. Trainees, together with their employers, choose the appropriate certificate. It could, for example, be an Intermediate Certificate in Wines, Spirits and Other Alcoholic Beverages or an Advanced Certificate in Food and Drink Service.

There is no set time period for completing the training programmes. The average time is three years, but some people take longer and others take less time.

Foundation Modern Apprenticeships (England), National Traineeships (Wales) and Skillseekers in Scotland are programmes for 16 and 17 year olds. Trainees work towards NVQ/SVQ Level 2 and train for the most junior jobs in the industry.

Advanced Modern Apprenticeships (England), Modern Apprenticeships (Wales) and some Skillseekers programmes in Scotland lead to NVQ/SVQ Level 3. They are intended for people between the ages of 16 and 25 who have completed Level 2 training or have GCSEs or even A-levels. At this level you would be aiming for a career as a supervisor or junior manager or you might choose to go on to a course in higher education.

What would you learn on a training programme?

Introductory skills, such as:

- basic job skills
- health, safety and hygiene
- customer care.

Followed by specialist skills in, for example:

- food preparation and cookery
- fast food
- reception.

Plus general skills:

- numeracy
- working with others
- IT
- problem solving.

You can get information on work-based training programmes from local offices of:

- careers companies
- Connexions Partnerships
- job centres
- the Learning and Skills Council (England)
- the National Council for Education and Training for Wales
- local enterprise companies (Scotland).

Stages

Still following the employment route, one method of training to become a chef – but one which requires a certain amount of self-confidence, not to mention initiative – is to arrange a series of *stages* (French for training period) and work through the different sections of a traditional kitchen (in different establishments and learning from different chefs). Some famous chefs have done exactly that. Well-known restaurant and hotel kitchens receive constant requests from would-be trainees, so to do this you would have to be very persistent and persuasive.

FULL-TIME COLLEGE COURSES

Nearly all the jobs at semi-skilled, skilled and supervisory levels in the hospitality industry can be entered by this route. Colleges of further education and some specialist catering colleges provide one- and two-year courses which incorporate NVQs/SVQs and lead to positions in the industry.

What are the advantages of this route?

- You have more time to learn and practise skills. You do not always have to work under the pressure of a real workplace situation. (In the early part of the course you can learn to cook dishes for example that will not be required for a specified time – ie guests are not waiting for them in a restaurant. Later, you will do them under real conditions.)
- Your training needs come first. The purpose of a college is to train people. It does not have to make a profit and put the customers' needs first.

And the drawbacks?

- You are not paid.
- There will be some expense involved – for equipment and visits.
- Some employers do not recruit from college courses.

The courses teach all the skills that an employee would acquire in a job. The difference is that there is some classroom work. Students are taught the theory behind a task before they go on to practise it. But there is a good deal of practical experience. Courses are far from being completely theoretical. Teaching staff have experience and qualifications in the hospitality industry themselves and know the working environment students will be entering. Practical experience comes in two ways.

- In the college. There will be, for instance, a reception desk staffed by students on a reception course, a kitchen organised into traditional sections where food preparation students prepare the meals which are served by food service students in a restaurant open to members of the public. The restaurant will be open at lunchtime and on some evenings – and may cater for evening functions and special dinners for local organisations.
- On work experience. Colleges arrange work experience placements with employers in the industry. Some colleges offer their students the

chance to do one placement in another country. Placements usually last for several weeks so that students get experience of working different shifts in real situations. Colleges also often arrange shorter specialist blocks of work experience and take their students to work at national events like the Chelsea Flower Show or the Derby.

Many students gain experience in a third way – through part-time jobs. They work in pubs, restaurants and hotels and are actively encouraged to do so by college lecturers. Some spend the Christmas period working as temporary live-in staff in hotels.

It is true that some employers prefer to train their own staff from scratch and do not recruit from college courses. The majority, however, do recruit from such courses. They provide top-up training in their own methods and usually regard students as trainees for a short period until they have proved that they can work both competently and speedily. Julien Hantonne (see page 32) has just finished a training period in a hotel and been promoted to waiter.

What kind of college courses can you take?

NVQ courses

These are available in all the main areas of work in the hospitality industry – just as they are in other employment. Examples of course titles include:

NVQ1 in Hospitality and Catering. One year.
(No formal entry requirements.) This leads to: employment or to a further course – NVQ 2.

NVQ2 in Hospitality and Catering or NVQ2 in Reception Studies. One year.
(Entry requirements: NVQ1; equivalent qualifications; or relevant experience.) This leads to: employment or to a NVQ3 course.

NVQ3 in Hospitality and Catering. One year.
(Entry requirements: NVQ2 or considerable experience.) This leads to supervisory work and junior management.

Advanced Vocational AS and A-level courses in Hospitality and Catering

What are they?

Advanced Certificates of Vocational Education (AVCE) are qualifications at the same level as AS and A-levels in academic subjects but organised differently. You could take a six-unit course which would give you one AS or A-level or a 12-unit one known as a double award. Students who were sure that they wanted to enter the hotel and catering industry would choose the double award. (Others might choose a six-unit course to test their liking for the industry and take other subjects at the same time.) The double award equates to NVQ/SVQ3 or two A-levels/three Highers and normally takes two years' full-time study.

Vocational AS and A-level courses in Hospitality and Catering can serve a useful purpose in providing a good introduction to the industry without forcing students to specialise. They keep their options open by preparing them in a *broad career area*, unlike NVQs and SVQs which are specific to particular jobs. So, on a course in Hospitality and Catering, you would cover the four main operational areas of food and drink preparation, food and drink service, accommodation and front office operations, rather than concentrating on one of them. The courses also contain general skills in communication, numeracy and using information technology. They are assessed through a combination of coursework and assignments plus externally set tests.

Students from Certificate of Vocational Education (VCE) A-level courses have several options. They can:

- begin employment in a chosen area;
- become a trainee on a junior management training scheme; or
- progress to a higher education course.

All colleges expect students to purchase some equipment when they start their courses. The usual requirement is a set of knives, chefs' and waiters' uniforms, and shoes with safety soles for kitchen work. Average outlay is £150. There will also be a requirement to contribute to the cost of some visits to employers' establishments and food fairs and exhibitions.

HIGHER EDUCATION COURSES

Increasingly, managers in the hotel and catering industry now have a higher education qualification, either a degree or a higher national diploma (HND).

What is the difference between them? Does it matter which you choose? Do they lead to the same kinds of job?

An HND course approaches most subjects from a management or operational angle. For example management accounts and operational marketing may be studied, whereas equivalent subjects within a degree programme could be management economics and strategic planning. Degree courses do not neglect operational management topics but most of them contain more theoretical subjects.

As far as jobs are concerned, most employers do not differentiate much between graduates – who have degrees – and diplomates (the title given to holders of diplomas) *at entry level*. Some large hotel groups will only consider graduates but many others, including some well-known names, accept applications from both and use their selection procedures to decide who to recruit.

However, because of the differing emphasis of degree and diploma programmes, graduates often move more quickly through companies' management training programmes or find it easier to move into jobs which have a more strategic role, eg development, planning and marketing.

You might want to take the following points into consideration when choosing between the two courses:

- Diploma courses are one year shorter.
- Entry grades are higher for degree courses.
- Degree courses contain more examinations and more essays to be written for both coursework and examinations. Students are also normally expected to research and write a dissertation.

However, many institutions allow transfer from one level of course to the other – in either direction – if students begin to feel that they have made a mistake.

And students who choose the diploma route for whatever reason can, if they wish, take a 'top-up' course to convert their diploma into a degree, or enter the final year of a degree course, should they eventually decide to do so.

Higher National Diploma courses

HNDs are two- or three-year courses which have an entry requirement of one A-level/two Highers or NVQ/SVQ Level 3. Approved equivalent qualifications and experience may be acceptable. The A-level need not be the vocational one in Hospitality and Catering. Almost any subject is accepted. Entry grades vary in different institutions. The more popular places might ask for the A-level to be at B or C grade for instance.

The courses are offered in colleges and universities and have a range of different titles. It is important to look at course content very carefully and make sure that you are choosing the one with the right emphasis. You could choose from:

- Culinary arts
- European hospitality management
- Hotel, catering and hospitality management
- Hotel and catering management.
- Hospitality management.
- Hotel management with tourism
- International hospitality management – and others
- Licensed trade management.

Foreign languages may be included and it is often possible to do some of the work experience in another country.

Courses are two years full time or three if they are sandwich courses including one year's industrial placement. In the hospitality industry, practical work experience is regarded as essential, so many courses are of the sandwich variety. Some of them are not, but teaching staff arrange their students' work experience in blocks consisting of perhaps one term plus the summer vacation.

Colleges and universities offering HND courses are free to design their own programmes, so content can vary considerably. They do, however, receive guidelines from either Edexcel (formerly the Business and Technology Education Council) or SQA, the Scottish Qualifications Authority. These are two validating bodies that monitor the quality of courses and award the diploma.

Degree courses

Degree courses are held in universities and colleges. They are three years full time or four if they are sandwich courses. Entry requirements are either two A-levels/three Highers, or NVQ/SVQ Level 3. Other approved equivalent qualifications and experience are sometimes accepted. Entry grades vary in different institutions. As is the case with HND courses, a very popular university or college can ask for more than the minimum qualifications.

Degrees are not awarded by external authorities like SQA or Edexcel but by the universities themselves. (Those offered in university colleges are usually validated by the partner university.) Universities and colleges are free to design their own courses, which, like the diploma courses, have different slants. Titles are similar to those of the HND courses.

Both degree and diploma course students have to learn and practise all the jobs in the hospitality industry. They take turns in working in the university or college's training kitchens and restaurants, just as students on NVQ courses do (see page 14) – although for shorter periods of time. And, of course, they get experience of all kinds of jobs while on practical placement.

Postgraduate diploma courses

Some employers will accept management trainees who have taken any subject for their first degree, but the majority expect applicants to have a relevant qualification.

If you have done or are doing a non-relevant course therefore, you might want to consider what is effectively a conversion course. These last for one year and are offered in a number of universities. Students study the same topics as those included in first degree courses and are also expected to carry out assignments, undertake a project and write a long essay or dissertation on a research topic.

Students who choose this route would be expected to have relevant experience and to be able to prove a strong interest in and knowledge of hotel and catering businesses. For this reason, it may be advisable to postpone the course for a year and to arrange some work experience in the industry. By doing so you would be sure that this was the right career choice and that the cost of further study would be a worthwhile investment. You would also be well prepared for application forms and interviews.

Postgraduate degree courses

A large number of these are also available – on both taught and research-based programmes. They lead to the award of an MA or MSc degree or to a PhD. However, like degrees in all subjects they are nearly all intended for people who already have a relevant first degree or appropriate experience which can be approved as equivalent.

THE PRIVATE SECTOR

If you can afford it, you may want to study hotel management at a private college. These vary in cost. Some can be very expensive – especially the world-famous ones in Switzerland. Their students usually gain jobs in the very best establishments though.

Another alternative if you want to concentrate on food preparation is to take a course at a private cookery school. Many of these are excellent – and again expensive. A number of private schools up and down the country offer courses that vary in length from one month to one year. It is very, very important to check carefully what kind of career path they are training their students for before you enrol. (It is very easy to find out by reading their prospectuses and arranging a visit.)

Some schools run three separate courses. The first covers the basic skills of cookery and the different cooking techniques. Students who wish to learn more enrol for the next one or two courses to work towards the school's own intermediate and advanced diplomas. Many also offer intensive four- to five-week courses for people who hope to work as chalet cooks in ski resorts or for students who hope to make use of cookery skills in a gap year.

The main difference between this type of training and that followed by a chef is that students learn to prepare entire meals for fairly small numbers of people, rather than to work in kitchens organised in traditional sections. They also learn to prepare buffets and cater for functions and receptions. The main career openings therefore are to work as private cooks, freelance caterers and cooks in smaller establishments with non-traditional kitchens. Having said that, there are always exceptions! Some former cookery school students *are* working in hotel and restaurant kitchens.

THE COST OF COLLEGE AND UNIVERSITY COURSES

Training costs in the state system are much more modest. Courses at further education level should cost very little for full-time students under 19 who should not have to pay tuition fees. Students over this age usually pay a few hundred pounds. As mentioned earlier, you must expect to pay for some visits organised as part of the course – and there will be travel costs to and from college.

Students on higher education courses may have to make a contribution towards tuition fees – which at present is a maximum sum of £1,100 each year. Contributions are assessed on family income. Some students make the full contribution; others (about 50 per cent) pay nothing. It is worth knowing that students who live in Scotland and attend Scottish universities and colleges pay no tuition fees. They do though pay a one-off sum, a graduate endowment – currently £2,000 – when they have qualified and are at work. Then there are living costs to be considered. Most students take out official student loans to help with these.

Students on all types of course usually have to purchase some equipment at the beginning – uniforms for both food preparation and food service, shoes and a set of knives.

If you are thinking about doing a full-time course you should never be put off initially by the cost. Colleges and universities have funds available to assist students in need and there are also some government bursaries for students on certain income levels. It is always worth enquiring from a college just how much help might be available.

Chapter 3
CAREER PATHS

It is very common to change jobs several times during a career spent in hotels and catering. People may do so either to gain experience in different types of job before deciding which is the right one or to set out deliberately to gain experience at different levels and with different employers before applying for management positions.

Most people have a preferred *area* of work though. Someone who is very keen on cookery is unlikely to train first in housekeeping, or a would-be receptionist to start in a kitchen. To make it easier to find out about the different jobs, brief overviews follow, divided into three main categories.

FOOD PREPARATION AND COOKERY

Catering manager

See **Food and Drink Services**.

Chalet cook

Holiday operators running ski holidays employ cooks to do all the catering (and sometimes the housekeeping too) for parties of skiers. The cooks provide a cooked breakfast, afternoon tea – with home-made cakes in the afternoon when the guests return from the slopes – and then, in the evening, a high-standard three- or four-course dinner. If there are children in the party, the cook may provide an early supper for them, with a different menu.

Cooks may cater for a small number of guests or for up to thirty. In the larger chalets it is more usual to have a separate a housekeeper and there may also be an assistant cook.

Skills required

- Ability to create different menus and provide meals of a high standard
- Flexibility.

Entry routes

- Any of the methods described under Chef.
- Taking a shorter course at a private cookery school which concentrates on teaching students to prepare an entire menu for a limited number of diners rather than giving them training in a traditional restaurant kitchen. (Many advertise *chalet cook* courses.)

Career prospects

Some chalet cooks become area or country managers for their employers or move into general tourism and become resort reps.

Chef

The word 'chef' is French for chief or boss – and a chef is someone in a position of responsibility in a kitchen. There are different grades and specialisms a chef can work in, and in order to understand them it is helpful to know how a large kitchen is organised.

A traditional restaurant kitchen is organised into sections, known by their French names (eg *partie* for section) as in the following diagram.

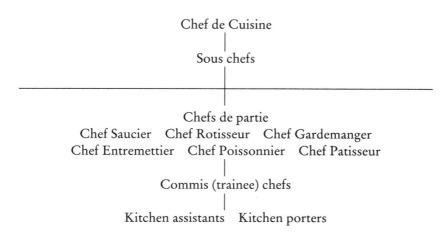

Chef de Cuisine

Sous chefs

Chefs de partie
Chef Saucier   Chef Rotisseur   Chef Gardemanger
Chef Entremettier   Chef Poissonnier   Chef Patisseur

Commis (trainee) chefs

Kitchen assistants   Kitchen porters

Saucier –	prepares meat, game and poultry dishes.
Rotisseur –	prepares roasted, fried and grilled meat.
Gardemanger –	prepares raw meat and poultry, cold dishes and starters.
Entremettier –	prepares eggs, vegetables and pasta.
Poissonnier –	prepares fish.
Patissier –	prepares bread, pastries and desserts.

Sous or senior chefs are fully qualified and experienced and are capable of working in any section of the kitchen. *Chefs de partie* run different sections and have their own staff. *Commis* or trainee chefs spend periods in all the sections as part of their training.

Chefs are capable of preparing an entire meal or any stage of it. However, if they work in a large kitchen organised as in the above chart, they will not prepare all the courses of a meal but instead will specialise in one section of a kitchen. On the other hand, private chefs – those working for individual employers and often those working in very small establishments – will cook the whole meal. Their training teaches them to cook all kinds of meals including classic French recipes, traditional English ones and dishes from all over the world.

Chefs prepare the food for the menu they have planned in advance or from one prepared by the head chef. They may draw up two kinds of menu, a set menu which offers a certain number of choices for a fixed price and a second (à la carte) one in which a larger number of dishes are priced individually. The set menu often remains the same for a period of time and incorporates ingredients that will be available throughout the period. The other may change according to what the chef finds is available in the markets. In small establishments they may shop daily, visiting a market and local shops. Chefs employed in bigger kitchens may do most of their ordering by telephone. Some will be restricted by their employers to using certain suppliers. Large hotels and hotel groups, for example, are able to negotiate substantial discounts because of their purchasing power through buying large quantities. Chefs usually establish good relationships with food suppliers, who value their regular custom.

Skills required

- Practical cookery skill
- Creativity

- Manual dexterity
- Stamina
- Ability to stand for long periods of time
- Ability to stand working in high temperatures
- Ability to remain calm in a crisis. (However, some chefs are notorious for not doing so and for losing their tempers when things are going wrong!)

Entry routes

- A traditional apprenticeship in a kitchen, with day release to a college of further education or to a specialist catering college for further training. (Many employers now use the Modern Apprenticeship programmes available.)
- A full-time course at college to obtain NVQ Levels 1 and 2, followed by full-time employment in a kitchen. (If you choose this route, you would be regarded as a trainee chef for a while until you had learned to work at speed and had learned the kitchen's way of doing things.)
- An Advanced Modern Apprenticeship, Modern Apprenticeship or National Traineeship. (Titles vary in England, Wales and Scotland.)

Career prospects
see Head chef.

Cook

The definitions of cook and chef overlap and can blur. However, the term cook is used more often by people working in schools, colleges, canteens, hospitals, residential homes and in private households. (There are some jobs known as *private chef* positions however.) People who cook for private functions, lunches and dinner parties are often known as cooks, but again the terms can be interchangeable. Cooks may prepare meals to very high standards and have generous budgets – or they may be expected to perform miracles on very tight budgets. It all depends where they work.

Cooks who work in industry, commerce and schools have more regular hours and are often employed up to and including lunchtime.

Skills required
The same as those for a chef.

Entry routes

- Cooks may train by any of the methods outlined under Chef.
- Alternatively, some take short courses at private cookery schools. (This is an option often taken by people wishing to work in chalets in ski resorts or as cooks in private households.)

Career prospects
Cooks' salary and promotion prospects are similar to those of chefs, although they are unlikely to reach the highest salaries of the top chefs.

Head chef

The head chef or *Chef de Cuisine* is head of the kitchen. Depending on the size of the kitchen, head chefs could be in charge of up to 30 staff, including qualified chefs, kitchen assistants/porters and trainee or apprentice chefs. They are responsible for budgeting, planning menus, ordering supplies and purchasing equipment, as well as organising staff rotas.

They have to ensure that the quality of the food is of a high standard and that all staff working in the kitchen follow food hygiene and safety regulations.

Training junior staff is also an important part of the job.

Skills required
These are the same basic ones as for a chef but with important additions. Running a large kitchen requires not only cooking skill but also the ability to manage a team of staff. In a hotel, the head chef is also a member of the management team and works closely with other managers, such as restaurant and conference and banqueting managers.

Entry routes
Head chefs usually have experience as chefs de partie, running several sections of a kitchen in a large hotel or restaurant. They may also have worked in a large kitchen as deputy head chef. Many head chefs have NVQ/SVQ Level 4.

Career prospects

A chef could move into management (perhaps as a food and beverage or catering manager) open a restaurant, move into teaching or even become a television celebrity chef!

CASE STUDY

Head Chef, Sean Ennis

Sean works in a medium-sized hotel, the Winchester Moat House, in Hampshire, which has 72 bedrooms, a restaurant and a leisure centre, organises banquets for up to 200 clients and employs 70 staff. He explains that whereas a larger kitchen would be divided into the traditional six sections, his, being smaller has three: Sauces, Larder and Desserts. Most of the main courses are prepared by Sauces. Staff are assigned to one section at the beginning of each shift but there is some movement between them according to the demands of the menu. Sean himself generally floats between all three sections, helping out where the pressure is greatest.

His responsibilities are:

- managing the budget
- planning the menus
- drawing up staff rosters
- training
- health and safety.

Sean plans the menus to suit the regular clients' tastes – which he has come to know well – and around what seasonal produce is available. (He orders from suppliers employed by the hotel group rather than using local suppliers and markets.) The basic menu changes every six months, but contains a number of daily specials. Sean uses a cosmopolitan selection of dishes, including French, Italian and Thai specialities. He discusses his menu ideas with his chefs and accepts ideas and input from them. The final menu is discussed with the food and beverage manager and the hotel operations manager.

Sean has a team of five full-time qualified chefs, two full-time kitchen porters and five part-time porters. The number at work at any one time varies according to the time of day and the workload. On average, three chefs and one kitchen porter will be on duty together. The fact that Sean's second and third chefs are experienced and competent means that he can confidently leave one of them in charge when he is not on duty.

'We have reasonable shifts here,' he says. 'People do ten shifts each week. There are four shifts in the day: 6am–10.00am; 10.00am–2.00pm; 2.00pm–6pm and 6pm–10pm. The afternoon shift is not normally very busy unless we have a buffet or wedding reception to prepare. People normally do two shifts a day, which could be consecutive or may have to be split if they are rostered for breakfast and dinner.

Split shifts are often unpopular and cause recruitment problems throughout the industry, but I am lucky in that the make-up of my team enables me to give staff their preferences for much of the time. I have one member for instance who prefers to work late and another who likes to work three shifts in a day and take an extra half day off.'

Training takes up a considerable part of Sean's time since he normally has one or two 'raw recruits' – apprentices who are training in the kitchen and attending college on day release. At the moment, he has one trainee chef whom he promoted from kitchen porter and another chef who has completed a full-time catering course and who worked for Sean on a part-time basis while a student. He is now finishing off his training as a full-time trainee.

Health and safety also takes up a lot of time, either from Sean or from one of the chefs. 'Food safety legislation now puts many requirements on us. We have to formally record so much that we have huge files of paperwork. For example, we have to record the temperature of the fridges, of cooked items and of deliveries. There might be as many as six deliveries of supplies each day. Someone has to check and record the suppliers' hygiene standards – that the driver was wearing disposable gloves, that his vehicle had separate departments for pre-cooked and fresh food.'

Sean's career history

Sean says that that mobility is essential if a chef is to progress and to find the right type of job to suit personal preferences. He has been a head chef since the age of 19 and has also found the time to contribute a chapter in a cookery book and prepare food for photography in magazine articles.

'I took the apprenticeship route. I actually wanted to be a butcher but there were no vacancies, and so when the careers officer suggested I became an apprentice chef I decided to give it a try. I trained for three years in a 30-cover restaurant near Milton Keynes. I then became the second chef. Next, I moved to become the head chef of a 46-bedroom country club in Wiltshire. I was there for two years, but I had little social life and so took the opportunity to move to a 20-cover restaurant in mid-Wales. I went from there to work in a very exclusive restaurant in Cardiff. I was there only six months because I saw an advertisement for the job of private chef in the Napa Valley, California. I applied and was successful.

'The California job was very interesting and different from any job I had had before. I was working for the owners of a winery. Part of my job was to plan menus to be served to wine tasters and prospective buyers. This meant devising recipes that enhanced the various wines. This is the complete opposite of normal meal planning when the wines are chosen to complement the food! I had to do a lot of research and practise using different flavours and textures around the three main styles my employers preferred – Oriental, Italian and French. It was very good experience; I learned a lot about wine. It was very much a case of "Taste this wine, then see what you can come up with". I soon learned for instance that tarragon brings out the buttery taste of Chardonnay. California was an interesting experience but was a fixed one-year contract, so I came back to look for another job. This time I was offered a job in a small country house hotel that was just being established. I stayed there five years. Then I decided to go for a new challenge and found a job in a larger hotel. But that entailed split shifts and a round journey of 120 miles. I have been in my present job for two and a half years now and enjoy it. I am given my budget and targets – and am then free to decide what I do and to run my kitchen as I wish. (I am not one of these old fashioned chefs who yells and screams at everyone, although everyone's temper can get a bit frayed under pressure.)'

Kitchen assistant

Kitchen assistants are semi-skilled staff who help in the preparation of meals under the supervision of the chef. Their duties include cleaning, peeling and slicing vegetables, skinning and gutting fish, and chopping meat, etc. Some of this may be done by hand, but kitchens have industrial-sized machines to help with much of the routine work – such as peeling and chipping potatoes.

The work also includes: clearing away, cleaning equipment and crockery by hand, operating washing-up machines, cleaning and scouring work surfaces and floors. Some kitchen assistants may cook simple items and may prepare all the tea and coffee orders. Unloading deliveries and taking supplies to and from store rooms may be part of the job where no kitchen porters are employed.

Skills required

- Stamina
- Flexibility
- Physical fitness
- Ability to stand for long periods of time.

Entry route
There are no minimum entry requirements and training is carried out in the kitchen.

Career prospects
Kitchen assistants who are prepared to train and work for NVQs could hope to be promoted to trainee chef. They might also choose to move into another catering job like food service or bar work.

Kitchen porter

Porters do some of the work of a kitchen assistant – normally the non-cooking duties described above.

Skills required

- Stamina
- Flexibility
- Physical fitness
- Ability to carry heavy loads.

Entry route

There are no minimum entry requirements and training is carried out in the kitchen.

Career prospects

A keen and committed kitchen porter could train as a chef.

School meals organiser

See **Food and Drink Services**.

Short order cook

The term 'short order cook' is often given to people who work in snackbars, takeaways and fast food outlets and cook a limited range of food.

Skills required

The same as those for a chef.

Entry route

Short order cooks are trained on the job by their employers.

Career prospects

These are similar to those of a chef.

FOOD AND DRINK SERVICES

Staff who work in the food and beverage departments of hotels and in restaurants, wine bars and canteens are front-line staff whose work always brings them into contact with customers.

The obvious jobs that spring to mind are those of the people who serve customers at the table and we will look at these jobs first before examining managerial-level careers on page 37.

Banqueting staff

Waiters and waitresses who serve guests at large functions usually work in hotels, which have function rooms for private parties and events. Unlike other food service staff they do not normally take meal orders from guests, as the menu has usually been agreed in advance and the same food is served to everyone. They do, however, have to be skilled in silver service, and they may take orders at each table for wine and other drinks and serve them.

Normally, they will be required to lay up the tables before the function and to clear away afterwards.

Many banqueting staff are employed as 'casuals', ie employed when needed to work with the permanent staff.

Skills required
The same as those for a waiter/waitress.

Entry route
As for waiter/waitress. No particular qualifications are required. Employers train their own staff.

Career prospects
There are prospects for banqueting staff to reach a head waiter's position.

CASE STUDY

Waiter, Julien Hantonne

Julien, who is French and comes from Paris, is currently working at the Lainston House Hotel, a four-star establishment in the Hampshire countryside.

How did he decide on a career in food service?

'The head waiter at the Crillon (a famous hotel in Paris) is a family friend and had told me a lot about the work and about meeting famous clients. I liked the sound of a job that would bring me into contact with customers and I could see that it would also give me the opportunity to travel. I asked a teacher at my school if he thought I would be suitable. He said "Yes" and suggested that I get some work experience to try out the work.'

So Julien found a job for one evening a week in a restaurant. He did like the work and decided to train for it as soon as he could. He left school at 16 and enrolled on a two-year course at a private catering school, the Ecole Hotelière Ferrandi in Paris. During the course he learned about food, the content of different dishes and sauces, cheeses, wines, other drinks, cocktails and how to serve them all. He also learned how to cook flambé dishes at the table in front of the customer. There was plenty of practice as the school had its own training restaurant where members of the public came to eat and be served by the students.

How did he come to be working in England?

I decided that I ought to improve my English if I wanted to be able to work in different countries. I asked staff at my college for advice and they contacted the head waiter here who is a former student. He arranged for me to come to Lainston House as a commis de rang or junior waiter. (The hotel uses French job titles.) It was a great opportunity and as the hotel provides accommodation I had no worries about finding somewhere to live. I have my own room in the staff block.'

As a commis or junior waiter, Julien carried trays of food to and from the kitchen and assisted a waiter in the restaurant. It was good experience he says, but he had no responsibility – 'I simply did as I was told.' After six months the restaurant manager told him that he was ready for promotion to chef de rang or waiter if he would like the job. 'There was no question. I was thrilled and rang my parents in Paris at once to tell them.'

He has been a chef de rang for just a few weeks and loves the work. 'I am in direct contact with guests now and it is up to me to make sure that they enjoy their meal – by answering any questions about the menu or suggesting a wine to accompany a particular dish if asked. I have to know everything about each dish on the menu – how it is cooked, which ingredients are in the sauces and to know about the wines we serve and which ones go well with each dish.' Julien is particularly interested in cheese. He has even bought three books on cheeses and enjoys being able to tell guests where each one comes from, what type of milk it is made from and how it has been made.

He works in a shift system, of five different shifts: breakfast and dinner – 6.30am to 10.30am, then 6.30pm until 10.30pm or 11pm ('when the last guest goes'); lunch and dinner – 10.30am to 3pm, then 6.30pm onwards; 1pm to 10pm; 3pm until the end of dinner; or breakfast and lunch – 6.30am to 3pm. Two of the shifts involve serving afternoon tea. The restaurant manager posts up the rotas every Saturday so that the staff know what the following week's shifts will be and can plan their social lives around them.

What happens on a typical shift?

'Breakfast is different because people are ordering a limited range of things and my main duties are to bring the order, then make sure that I keep them supplied with tea, coffee and toast. The other two meal services are more interesting! There are two restaurants: one with seven tables, the other with eight. The head waiter looks after both, but each has one chef de rang and a commis de rang. Before the meal service begins I lay up the table, polish the glasses, cutlery and plates and make sure that I have supplies of bread, butter and water. The restaurant manager explains the menu to us – and we are ready. I take guests' orders – and remember each person's choices. (It is very unprofessional to have to ask again!) I make sure that they have the correct cutlery for the dishes they have ordered and serve the food as it is given to me by the commis.

'The skill is in serving every person at the right time when you might have several main courses arriving together and you have some tables eating starters while some are already on dessert. I also have to keep my eyes on the different tables and fill wine and water glasses or bring more bread. There is an art, too, to knowing how much or little to talk to the guests. You have to know when not to disturb a business conversation or to sense when some people do want to talk to you. A lot of people do talk to me because they hear my accent and want to know where I am from. After each course I ask if everything has been all right – but never more often. That was explained firmly to me at catering school, when I was so nervous that I kept asking if everything was OK all through the meal.'

Where will Julien go from here?

'I hope to be able to speak really good English in two years. Then I intend to go to Spain and spend one year learning Spanish. At the same time, of course, I will be gaining experience as a chef de rang. I want to move up the promotion structure – to head waiter then restaurant manager and I want to work in different countries. My ambition is to open my own bar in Paris eventually.'

Bar staff

Bar staff do much more than serve drinks and talk to customers. Before the bar opens they have to make sure that it is fully stocked – with wines, beers, spirits, etc (which means carrying and changing barrels), but also with ice, lemons and whatever nibbles are offered. They check optics, spirits dispensers and beer pumps. They also clean and tidy the bar area before opening time and after closing time, and at the end of a shift they cash up and balance the till. They may wash glasses. In some bars they are expected to mix cocktails.

Skills required

- Friendly manner – willingness to talk to customers
- A good memory
- Knowledge of the range of drinks
- Ability in mental arithmetic
- Ability to work at speed when the bar is full.

Entry routes

- Training is given on the job.
- Beverage service is included in full-time college courses in catering.
- There is a minimum age of 18 *except* for young people aged 16 and 17 who are taking part in an approved Modern Apprenticeship programme. They are allowed to work behind a bar.

Career prospects
Experienced bar staff can become pub managers or run their own pub.

Commis

Commis or junior waiters are employed in most restaurants. Their duties include clearing tables and often setting them under supervision, and bringing dishes from the kitchen to a separate area for collection by the waiters. Commis are often trainee waiters but the job can be done as a permanent position.

Skills required
The same as those for a waiter/waitress.

Entry route
As for a waiter/waitress. No particular qualifications are required. Employers train their own staff. Some employers prefer to start people

who have completed college courses as commis waiters initially and promote them to waiter as soon as they are ready. See the profile of Julien Hantonne who entered by this route.

Career prospects

There are prospects for a commis to reach the position of head waiter.

Head waiter/waitress

A head waiter/waitress is in charge of customer service and a team of food service staff. They must keep an eye on the table service and ensure that dishes are served as they appear from the kitchen. They do some waiting themselves and in some restaurants cook certain dishes at the table. In some restaurants they also act as restaurant manager.

Skills required

- Organisational ability
- Leadership
- Outgoing personality.

Entry routes

Head waiters/waitresses are promoted from trained and experienced waiting staff.

Career prospects

A head waiter could become a restaurant manager – and from there, if working in a hotel, could progress to food and beverage manager.

Waiter/waitress

(In some restaurants the title waiter is used for both male and female staff.)

The work of a waiter/waitress starts before the customers arrive. At the beginning of a shift they lay tables with tablecloths, napkins, glasses and cutlery and put menus on tables. They welcome customers, take their orders – answering any questions or advising on dishes – and pass the orders to the kitchen. (In some restaurants the orders are taken by the

head waiter.) As they take the orders they make a note of the food
ordered by each guest (often using a small table seating plan on their
order pads), as it is unprofessional for a good waiter to need to ask for
the guests' choices again. They may then bring different cutlery
according to the type of food ordered. They serve the guests and present
the bill at the end of the meal. Sometimes they deal with the bill; often
they take it to a cashier. Before they leave at the end of a shift they clear
the tables. If they are employed in a hotel they may set tables for
breakfast at the end of an evening shift.

There are two different types of meal service: silver service when the
waiter/waitress serves the food on to guests' plates from dishes or
platters, and plated service when the food comes from the kitchen
already on the plates.

Skills required

■ Physical fitness
■ Ability to be on feet for long periods and to carry heavy dishes
■ Manual dexterity.

Entry routes

■ On-the-job training as a junior waiter
■ Full-time college course in general catering with food service included.
  Modern Apprenticeship/National Traineeship route.

Career prospects

There are prospects for waiters/waitresses to reach the position of head
waiter.

Wine waiter

Wine waiters (or sommeliers) are normally employed only in larger
restaurants. They are expected to be knowledgeable about different wines,
vintages and liqueurs and to be able to advise customers on appropriate
wines to accompany their meals. Their duties also include storing wines at
correct temperatures and in correct conditions. In some restaurants the
head wine waiter may assist in the selection and purchase of wines.

Skills required

- Knowledge of wines and other drinks
- Friendly and helpful manner.

Entry routes

It is usual to specialise in this work after experience in food and drink service. NVQs are available, as are courses organised by the Wine and Spirit Educational Trust.

Career prospects

This is a specialist job, undertaken by trained waiters. There are prospects of working as a wine waiter in larger restaurants or moving back into general waiting and being promoted from there. Prospects are as for waiter/waitress.

Managerial-level careers

Catering manager

Catering managers are responsible for the provision and service of meals within an organisation. They handle budgets, plan menus, order supplies, recruit, train and manage staff, monitor standards, and make sure that staff follow food hygiene and safety procedures. This job is very similar to that of a food and beverage manager but the term is more often used in the non-profit making sector, ie in schools, hospitals, prisons, in the armed services and in employee canteens/restaurants, although it is also used in airlines and shipping companies. Managers normally have to work to very tight financial limits but as some institutions also cater for external functions, conferences and banquets, they and their staff do get the opportunity to produce some meals on more generous budgets. Universities and colleges, for instance, earn considerable income from conferences in vacations.

Contract catering managers work for companies that organise catering for functions, events, shows, promotional events and some private functions. They combine some of the duties of catering, food and beverage and banqueting managers, discussing requirements with the client and overseeing the entire process.

Skills required

- Leadership
- Numeracy
- Communication skills.

Entry routes

Catering managers often have Higher National Diplomas or degrees in hotel and catering/hospitality management or in institutional management in addition to experience.

Career prospects

Catering managers can move to bigger organisations or companies or into the hotel side of the industry and gain promotion to general management. See food and beverage manager.

CASE STUDY

Graduate Trainee Catering Manager, Marie Nix

Marie works in the in-house catering department at Liverpool Hope University College. The catering department serves 500 breakfasts and dinners each week day to resident students, and also provides a lunch service through a main refectory with several different serveries (a deli bar, a salad bar and one serving hot dishes), vending machines, a bar in the Students' Union and another for lecturers – who also have their own à la carte restaurant. The cash-take each lunchtime, says Marie, is around £2,500. The department also cooks meals for conferences held at the college during vacations. The staff consist of the catering and conference manager, her assistant manager, 12 chefs, two senior front-of-house supervisors, two supervisors and 40 front-of-house staff.

Although technically a trainee, Marie acts as the assistant catering and conference manager. This is excellent experience, she says. 'I am doing a real job but at the same time I am receiving some training. For example, I attend meetings and I sit in on a lot of what my boss does – recruitment or disciplinary interviews for instance.'

What does a typical day involve?

'I come in the morning and go straight to the refectory to see that the breakfast shift is going OK. Then it's to my office for a paperwork session. I do things like read and approve holiday request forms (checking staffing levels as I do so), deal with any maintenance requests and call appropriate repairers or service engineers, check stock levels and order all the confectionery, drinks and cakes for the vending machines. I'll probably also do a health and safety check, like making sure that all the cleaning materials are correctly labelled or walk round to see that there are no wet and slippery floors without warning notices. Then it's a case of what crops up. I might have some 'return from sickness' interviews to do. If someone comes back after an absence, I have to talk to them and ensure that they are fit to come back and have a doctor's certificate.

'Then it's lunchtime. I walk round to see that the bars are stocked, food is up to standard and being served quickly, that staff are all in uniform, the menu boards are correct and so on. After the cashiers have cashed up and I have checked their totals, I have my own lunch. The afternoon passes with more administrative work, perhaps some staff training and any one of several projects I am working on. Since I have been here I have introduced some different products that I knew were good from my experience in other establishments, and I have redesigned the bar areas and ordered new furniture for them. I have also done some staff training for new cashiers. I am currently writing a training pack for silver service staff at conferences to follow up some training I have done for them on correct ways to hold plates when serving and how to clear properly.'

What does Marie like about her job?

'The responsibility. My boss is willing to delegate and lets me use my initiative. Plus the regular hours. I work 9.00am to 5pm during the week – and from 10.00am until 2.30pm on one Saturday and Sunday each month.'

Marie's career history

While she was doing her A-levels, Marie had thoughts about teaching. However, a period of work experience soon put her off! She then decided that as she enjoyed her part-time job in a small hotel, she would train for a management career in the hospitality industry. She then did a degree course in Hotel and Catering Operations Management at Huddersfield University.

It was a four-year sandwich course, with the third year spent in industry. Marie felt that she already knew about work in hotels and opted instead to work in the education sector. She struck lucky with her placement at Buckinghamshire Chilterns University College, where she was given a good deal of responsibility and spent most of the year acting as deputy manager. On graduating, Marie was sure that she wanted to work in the education sector (and was even more convinced that she did not want the irregular and long hours involved in hotel work). She went for two interviews, was offered both jobs – and chose Liverpool Hope.

Conference and banqueting manager

A hotel's conference and banqueting manager co-ordinates different services within the hotel to organise functions for clients. Such functions could include: business meetings for a small group of people, wedding receptions, parties, banquets for 500 guests or conferences lasting several days. Each function will have different requirements but all will need the manager to pay great attention to detail to ensure that the client is satisfied and wishes to return to the hotel again. The conference and banqueting manager would first meet with the client, discuss what is required and perhaps make some suggestions. He or she would then confirm the arrangements to the client and agree the price.

After the conference and banqueting manager has agreed with the client the services to be provided, then comes the task of liaising with the managers whose departments will be involved in the event, discussing menu and bar requirements, numbers of staff required, furnishing of conference rooms, arrangements for hiring any additional equipment, providing live music and so on. The conference and banqueting manager or deputy attends many functions in person to make sure that everything runs smoothly.

Skills required

- Organisational ability
- Attention to detail
- Communication skill
- Flexibility.

Entry routes

Most conference and banqueting managers have previous experience in another management position within a hotel, often in food and beverage or front-of-house management.

Career prospects

As for food and beverage manager.

Fast food restaurant manager

The responsibilities of this type of restaurant manager extend to the kitchen as well as the restaurant itself. Since the menu is limited, the kitchen does not normally have a trained chef. The manager recruits and trains both cooking and serving staff and is responsible for the profitability of the entire restaurant or 'unit'. They might offer special events like children's parties. They often do cooking duties themselves and train new staff by working with them. They normally order all the food supplies from the restaurant chain's suppliers.

Skills required

- Leadership
- Numeracy
- Ability to train junior staff
- Communication skills.

Entry routes

- It is possible to start as a part-time or full-time catering or waiting assistant and be trained by the organisation and promoted. Training is provided by managers. Trainees often complete a workbook or training log as they learn how to do each task.
- Some of the major pizza and other fast food chains run management training programmes for graduates in any subject.

Career prospects

There are possibilities of becoming an area or regional manager, responsible for a number of restaurants. There are also opportunities to move into head office positions in marketing, training or human resources management.

Food and beverage manager

Food and beverage managers are usually responsible for the provision of food and drink throughout a hotel. This means that they must work closely with heads of food preparation and food service departments. Among their responsibilities are budgeting, ordering supplies (except in establishments where purchasing is done by the chef), supervising and monitoring standards, and training and developing staff. They normally hold daily meetings with heads of their different departments to discuss forward planning, special events, future promotions, profit and costs.

Skills required

- Leadership
- Numeracy
- Communication skills.

Entry routes

Food and beverage managers often have Higher National Diplomas or degrees in hotel and catering/hospitality management in addition to experience in various food and beverage departments.

Career prospects

This job is a traditional stepping stone on the route to a position as hotel general manager.

Pub manager/owner

Many pubs are run by tenants who rent the premises from a brewery and pay them a proportion of the profits; others by owners who have bought them outright. About 20 per cent are directly managed by the owners – usually chains and large breweries. In these companies, managers have a career structure and may move on to manage bigger pubs – or into area or regional management, marketing and training.

Whatever the system, the jobs of tenants, owners and managers are very similar. They are in charge of all aspects of serving alcoholic beverages, soft drinks and food. If the pub has a restaurant, they fulfil the duties of a restaurant manager. They must obey local licensing laws and any rules laid down by the brewery (for example, regarding which brands of food and drink may be served and what opening hours must be kept). They are responsible for recruiting and managing staff, many of whom are part time. In order to make the pub profitable, they often organise a range of activities – quizzes, sponsored events, theme nights, sometimes discos – and decide when to offer special deals, as in discounted meals and drinks to attract more customers.

Skills required

- Communication skill
- Managerial ability
- Friendly disposition

Entry routes

- Through promotion from bar work.
- Many of the large chains now run training schemes for graduates and holders of HNDs. Breweries run short training courses for tenants and managers.

Career prospects

Successful managers could expect to find openings in the company's management structure, as area or regional managers, responsible for a number of pubs or in head office positions in marketing, training or human resources management.

Restaurant manager

Restaurant managers are in overall charge of the running of a restaurant. They may help to plan menus in consultation with the chef and order some of the supplies. They are responsible for organising staff rotas, training staff, ensuring that food is handled hygienically and properly served. In a silver service type restaurant they train staff as waiters and waitresses. They may greet customers when they arrive and check that they have enjoyed their meal before they leave.

Restaurant managers often do some food service themselves and may cook some special dishes at the customers' table.

Skills required

- Communication skills
- Skill in dealing with customers
- Organisational ability
- Flexibility (and willingness to serve at tables if they are short-staffed).

Entry routes

- Managers of silver service restaurants usually have a background in food service and, often, experience as a head waiter.
- Some restaurant managers have diplomas or degrees in hotel and catering operations/management.

Career prospects

Restaurant managers could be promoted to area or regional manager in restaurant chains. If working in hotels, they could aim for promotion to food and beverage manager.

School meals organiser

School meals organisers are responsible for the catering in a number of schools. Some of the schools will have their own kitchens while others will have the meals delivered from a central kitchen. Organisers plan the menus, working usually to a tight budget and try to balance the difficult task of encouraging healthy eating with children's own tastes. They visit all their schools regularly and are responsible for recruiting and training their staff. They may sometimes accept additional business – like providing a lunch for a teachers' conference.

Skills required and entry routes
As for catering manager.

Career prospects
There is the possibility of promotion to senior manager, in charge of the school meals service for a local education authority. Other possibilities include catering or restaurant management positions in other non-profit-making establishments – or even crossing over into the commercial sector.

Other jobs not covered in this section

- Airline steward/ess
- Conference organiser
- Special events organiser
- Train steward/ess.

ACCOMMODATION SERVICES

These are the jobs directly related to looking after guests in establishments that provide overnight accommodation. Although people obviously stay in all kinds of establishments, such as guest houses and pubs, most of the jobs described are found only in hotels – and in the larger ones at that – since it is only in these that some of the more specialist jobs exist.

Hotels come in all types, shapes and sizes, from large four- and five-star establishments with hundreds of rooms plus restaurants, bars, shops, leisure clubs and business facilities, to smaller hotels with more limited facilities. Many have function suites for conferences and banquets. Some are part of national or international hotel groups, others are independently owned.

As with the previous section, these jobs are split into two lists, with managerial-level jobs starting on page 53.

Cabin steward (ship)

Stewards work on cruise ships – where they may be at sea for a long period of time. (Between each voyage they have a period of shore leave.) Their duties are similar to those of a room attendant on shore, but with some of those of a room service waiter and a general cleaner. They clean and service passenger cabins, bring early morning tea or coffee and newspapers, deliver light snacks ordered to cabins and clean the corridors adjacent to cabins.

Skills required

- Liking for practical work
- Ability to work methodically
- Physical fitness
- Friendly and helpful manner.

Entry routes

This is a very popular job which is difficult to enter without previous experience in a four- or five-star hotel.

Career prospects

An experienced cabin steward could become a chief steward.

Cashier

Some hotels employ cashiers to keep a running total of expenditure, prepare bills for guests who are leaving the hotel and take payments for all the hotel services they have used. Residents may, for example, have signed individual bills from room service or the restaurant for inclusion in their final account.

This might be a 'back room' job, or cashiers might be based in the reception area where they also deal with foreign currency exchange. It is necessary to understand the procedures for accepting cheques, credit card payments and travellers' cheques. They must also know how to operate a till and be able to deal with complaints and put right any mistakes.

Skills required

- Attention to detail
- Numeracy
- Friendly and helpful manner.

Entry routes

There are no formal entry requirements. Many cashiers train on the job. Some join hotels after previous experience of accounts or general office work.

Career prospects

A cashier could decide to train as a receptionist or move to bigger establishments in order to earn a higher salary as a cashier.

Head porter

A head porter (or concierge in some hotels) leads a team of porters responsible for carrying luggage, acting as messengers and providing information on the hotel services and facilities. They draw up staff rotas to provide 24-hour-a-day cover. Security considerations are very important and they work closely with a security manager where one is employed. During their stay, guests turn to the porters' desk for help with anything from arranging taxis and local transport to purchasing tickets for local attractions. Head porters or their assistants may book seats for theatres, exhibitions and sporting events and give advice on what visitors can see and do. They normally have an extensive knowledge of the local area including restaurants, theatres, shops, car hire services, sightseeing and entertainment.

Skills required

- Physical fitness
- Polite and helpful manner
- Local knowledge.

Entry routes
Through promotion from work as a porter.

Career prospects
A head porter is at the top of the career ladder – but might be able to improve both salary and conditions by changing employer.

Head receptionist

Many hotels have teams of receptionists, supervised by a head receptionist who draws up staff duty rotas and trains junior staff. They take part in the shift system themselves and share in the general work at the desk. They also deal with any queries that cannot be handled by their staff and handle any complaints.

Skills required and entry routes
See under Receptionist.

Career prospects
The most obvious promotion would be to front-of-house manager, but some receptionists might choose to move to other administrative jobs within a hotel or hotel group, such as sales and marketing or into conference and events management.

Housekeeper

Housekeepers are responsible for domestic services in hotels and in institutions such as hospitals and residential establishments.

They organise and check the work of room attendants, cleaners, and possibly laundry staff. They ensure that bedrooms and public areas are cleaned on time each day, that supplies of linen and items such as tissues, soap and cosmetics are available for re-stocking bathrooms, that routine and emergency maintenance is undertaken and that high standards of cleanliness and efficiency are achieved.

Their work involves: allocating daily cleaning duties, issuing keys, linen, and cleaning materials; inspecting rooms to ensure that all rooms have been thoroughly cleaned; arranging for maintenance work to be undertaken or for damaged items to be replaced. Housekeepers liaise closely with other hotel departments to ensure that guests' requests are dealt with speedily and efficiently.

In a large hotel, there may be a team of housekeeping staff, with a housekeeper in charge of one or more floors. In a smaller hotel one house-keeper may be responsible for all accommodation, including public rooms.

Skills required and entry routes
As for head housekeeper.

Career prospects
There is a career ladder in large hotels leading to positions of deputy and head housekeeper.

Porter

In large hotels, members of the porters' department may do specific jobs, for example, doorman, luggage porter and hall porter. In smaller establishments, duties will be shared. Porters normally carry guests' luggage to their rooms, show them to the room and explain how to use any equipment there. If they take a turn at working on the porters' desk, they come into much more contact with guests throughout their stay.

Skills required

- Friendly and helpful personality
- Physical fitness
- Smart appearance.

Entry routes
There are no formal entry requirements for this work but some hotels expect staff to be 18. Training is given by the head porter and senior porters.

Career prospects
Porters can ultimately become head porters or concierges.

Receptionist

Hotel receptionists are usually the first people that guests talk to, either in person or on the telephone, and they therefore have a major role in creating a favourable impression of the hotel. Their work involves accepting bookings for accommodation, either in writing, on the telephone, via the Internet or in person, greeting guests when they arrive, establishing how they wish to pay and verifying credit cards, issuing room numbers and keys or key cards, arranging for luggage to be taken to rooms, explaining the hotel procedures and answering any questions. They liaise with Housekeeping which informs them when rooms are cleaned and available. They answer guests' queries during their stay and may refer them to the porters' desk for further services. Receptionists may also work behind the scenes, preparing guests' bills (see further details under Cashier) and dealing with correspondence.

Skills required

- Friendly and helpful manner
- Ability to cope with pressure during busy periods
- A knowledge of one or more foreign languages is useful.

Entry routes

- A full-time college course leading to a diploma/certificate in hotel reception and front office work which includes NVQs/SVQs.
- Training in a hotel, including NVQs/SVQs.
- Modern Apprenticeship programme.

Career prospects

A receptionist can become a deputy head or head receptionist.

CASE STUDY

Hotel Receptionist, Beverley Hallett

Beverley works at the Winchester Moat House Hotel, where she was a room attendant until the operations manager recognised her potential and promoted her.

Her hours vary according to the shift she is on, either early (6.30am–3pm) or late 2.30pm–11pm. Sometimes the pattern means that she works a late shift followed by an early and therefore goes home to have 'just a couple of hours to myself before going to bed and then getting up to come back to work', but she does not mind this because she has found somewhere to live only ten minutes' walking distance from the hotel and the consecutive shifts are compensated for by several days off together. She knows what shifts she will be working one week in advance and if she has an important reason for wishing to be free at a particular time, she can enter that date on the calendar, so that the head receptionist is aware of it when drawing up the rosters.

On a typical day shift, her work starts with dealing with the overnight dockets from the bar and the night porter. These are the receipts guests have signed for food and drink purchases made after 11pm. Beverley's job is to check that they have been signed, then put the top copy with other bills accumulated under the guests' room numbers and send the second copy to the hotel's accounts department. The first guests could begin to check out within the next half hour. During the week, most are business travellers with appointments to keep and expect their bills to be ready when they hand in their room keys at the reception desk. The next hour could be very busy with several guests arriving at the desk to settle their bills, others coming with queries and the phone ringing. Beverley has to deal with them all, politely and competently – but this is a part of the job she enjoys. She loves working with people.

What else does the job involve?

'I check in arriving guests, ask them whether they will be paying in cash (in which case they pay in advance) or by credit card. If it is by card, I take an imprint of their card. I ask whether they will require a morning paper and wake-up call, give them the key to the room and explain how to get there. That is unless they need help with their luggage. If so, a porter takes it and shows them to the room. I take reservations by phone if the reservations manager is busy, answer any questions guests have and generally deal with anything that arises. Sometimes they ask advice on what to see in the area or for the telephone numbers of restaurants. I give them what information I can and usually give them a copy of the local tourist map and mark the sights they want to see on that. One thing I am not very good at doing is giving road directions because I don't drive myself and if someone says "How do I get to the motorway?", I am a bit stuck – but I am learning. And if I'm not sure, I ask one of the other staff. I also keep a check on the number of arrivals we expect, allocate rooms and make sure that I know how many vacant rooms we have. I phone all the other hotels in the area each day and check their situation so that if we are full when someone wants to make a reservation I can recommend an alternative. Typing up the restaurant menus is also one of my duties.

'Before the end of a shift I have to cash up and make sure that all the credit card slips in guests' names balance with the computer record. If there is a mistake, it can take a long time to find, so I hope that there won't be any. At the end of a shift, I close the accounts and put the cash in the safe – with the exception of £100. It is very important that we always have that amount as a cash float.'

Skills

Beverley says that a receptionist needs to be methodical and to understand the computer systems used. On the personal side, communication skills and patience are very important. Guests do complain from time to time, but they usually respond well, if you are polite and they can see that you are doing your best to sort out the problem.

Career path

When she left school, Beverley took a full-time course leading to an Intermediate Diploma in Business Administration at a college of further education. At that time, she was thinking about a business career or of joining the navy. As a student, she had a weekend job as a room attendant, first in another hotel, subsequently in the one where she works now. When she left college she became a full-time room attendant while working out what to do next.

'I worked here, learned how to do the job and was soon asked to act as assistant housekeeper on some shifts. When I heard that there was a vacancy for a receptionist, I applied, had the interview and was accepted. When the operations manager told me that I had been successful I was so pleased that I rushed back upstairs and ran shouting down the corridor!'

Beverley's training was carried out in the hotel by the head receptionist and lasted for about one month. 'I was so nervous on the first day – especially when the phone rang. At first, I worked the same shifts as the head receptionist, who said that I should watch her for the first shift and that she would gradually ease me into doing some of the work myself on the second. I am regarded as trained now, but I am still the junior – and I can always ask for help from the duty manager if I have a problem.'

Reservations staff

In large hotels, reception work is split into a number of different areas and specialist reservations staff will be employed.

This job involves taking advance reservations from individual guests, companies or travel agents, entering details onto the reservations computer and allocating rooms to guests. Staff must be careful to enter the guests' requirements – including the length of stay, type of room and any special requests such as for a non-smoking room. If guests have a guaranteed reservation and will be arriving late, it is also important to note this to ensure that their room is not allocated to someone else. Reservations may need to be confirmed in writing or by sending an e-mail or fax. Reservations staff may also do other clerical work associated with the reception area of the hotel.

Skills required

- Good keyboard skills
- Accuracy
- A good telephone manner.

Entry routes

- Through experience or training on a hotel reception course.
- Through experience in general office or reception work.

Career prospects

Reservations staff could move into reception desk work and up through the front-of-house career structure.

Room attendant

Room attendants clean and prepare guests' rooms in a hotel under the supervision of the housekeeper. They must work quickly and efficiently, since only a limited time is allowed for each room. Room attendants usually start by removing trays of used china and glasses, emptying litter bins and ash trays, and gathering up dirty linen before moving on to making beds, dusting, vacuuming and cleaning bathrooms. In most hotels, the majority of the work is done in the morning. However, in some larger and airport hotels, servicing of rooms is carried out throughout the day. In some hotels, room attendants do an evening duty, turning down bed covers in bedrooms. Room attendants usually work alone – and the work is physically demanding.

Skills required

- Liking for practical work
- Ability to work methodically
- Physical fitness.

Entry routes

There are no formal qualifications. Training is done on the job.

Career prospects

There is the possibility of promotion to housekeeping positions.

CASE STUDY

Beverley Hallett, Room Attendant

Beverley, who is now a hotel receptionist (see page 49) used to work as a room attendant (known in some hotels as *chambermaid*). She describes the work.

'The hours of work were 8am–4pm. I would come on duty in the morning and be given my list of rooms. That shows which ones will have guests checking out or arriving, with the number of guests and their names. Then I would go to my cupboard and collect all my cleaning equipment. There is a cupboard between every 16 rooms. As a regular member of staff, you have your own cupboard and are responsible for keeping it stocked. (When I ran out of anything, I just asked for the key to a shed outside the hotel where everything was kept and replaced what I needed.) Keeping your cupboard in order means that you can get to work more quickly, so you get very cross if someone else who has been using it while you are off duty leaves it in a mess!

'The length of time taken to clean a room depends on whether the guests have checked out – which means stripping and making up beds – and on the number of guests using it. A daily clean probably takes 25 to 30 minutes if you are organised. I soon worked out a daily routine. I would start by emptying the bins and removing all the rubbish, then I would do the bathroom and last, the bedroom. Making beds, dusting and vacuuming had to be done in every room every day and I would polish the furniture in some of the rooms each day. Finally, I would restock the bathroom with gels and soap and the hospitality tray with tea and coffee supplies.

'Fridays are often the busiest days because business guests are all checking out and a number of rooms need beds making up. But then weekends can bring families with extra beds and cots to be put in some rooms.

'It's hard work – and you have to go home to your own housework! And it's important work because guests won't come back if their room isn't properly cleaned and looking welcoming. An experienced attendant will work largely unsupervised but the housekeeper or assistant housekeeper will check the rooms.'

Managerial-level jobs

Front-of-house manager

Front-of-house managers are employed to run the reception and front office services which process arrivals, departures and handle any queries, requests or complaints from guests. They manage a team of receptionists, reservations staff, telephonists and office staff. The work includes setting up and maintaining systems for taking advance reservations and maintaining accurate records, setting standards for the reception that guests receive when arriving at the hotel, and managing the preparation of guests' bills. Front-of-house managers must plan ahead to ensure that sufficient staff are available to staff the reception area for seven days a week, particularly during the busy period in the mornings when guests are checking out.

Skills required

■ Communication skills
■ Ability to lead, train and motivate a team of staff
■ Knowledge of hotel, general office and computer systems
■ Ability to remain calm under pressure
■ Foreign languages are useful.

Entry routes

Front-of-house managers may have:

■ Experience of front office work
■ Experience of work at head receptionist level
■ Training gained on a management training scheme.

Many front-of-house managers have diplomas or degrees.

Career prospects

A front-of-house manager's logical progression would be to the same job in a larger hotel or moving sideways into another management job.

Head housekeeper

In large hotels, a head or executive housekeeper is responsible for a team of housekeepers, who in turn supervise room attendants, cleaners, and linen room staff. As a part of the management team of the hotel, head housekeepers are responsible for the implementation of health and safety regulations, the cleanliness of public rooms and bedrooms and for their equipment. They may also be involved in planning redecoration schemes, ordering supplies of cleaning materials and purchasing furnishings and equipment. Some are involved in planning decoration and colour schemes. They usually manage their own budgets and may negotiate prices with suppliers of equipment, florists and with laundries.

In the hospitality services sector, ie in hospitals, university halls of residence and residential homes, a head housekeeper may be known as a domestic services manager or domestic bursar. In hospitals they are responsible for cleaning all areas, including the wards – where a particular emphasis must be placed on hygiene, and special regulations on disposal of waste and avoidance of cross-infection must be observed.

Skills required

- Organisational ability
- Attention to detail
- Knowledge of cleaning and caring for furniture and fittings
- Physical fitness. (They spend much of their working day on their feet, walking round to inspect their staff's work.)

Entry routes

- Head housekeepers need experience working as housekeepers.
- Many have National or Higher National Diplomas or professional qualifications.

Career prospects

A head housekeeper could move into similar areas, such as domestic services management in a hospital or university residence.

CASE STUDY

Executive Housekeeper, Gwendael Ingouf

Gwendael is the executive housekeeper at Cardiff's Hilton Hotel where she manages 50 people – one senior supervisor, five other supervisors (including one working at night), room attendants, linen porters and cleaners for the public areas. She is very young to hold such a position (at 26), but then she is extremely well qualified.

Gwendael, who is French, obtained the baccalauréat (the equivalent of A-levels) at the age of 16 and therefore went to university two years early. She did a degree in business administration and languages at the Sorbonne University in Paris – and followed this with a master's degree in Business at a university in Germany. She then went to a university in the south of France to do a master's course in Hospitality and Tourism!

Why did she choose the hospitality business?

'Because I had had part-time jobs in hotels and enjoyed the work. I spent four months working as a chambermaid between school and university and I also spent a winter season working as a receptionist in a holiday centre in a ski resort. I had to do sandwich placements on my first degree course and for my first one chose to work in the hotel industry. I spent eight weeks in an Austrian hotel where I worked as a commis waiter and also translated all the menus into English and French. For the next one, I went to the Hotel Concorde Lafayette in Paris and worked there as a floor supervisor. During the placement I had to undertake a project – and reorganised all the administration in the housekeeping department. Basically, they were still working out staff duty rotas with pencil and paper. I produced a rota for the whole year so that staff knew exactly when their duty shifts, time off and holidays would be, and set it up as a computer system. That project gave me very good administrative experience and the work as a supervisor gave me experience in managing staff and helped me to see that the housekeeping side of hotel work could be an interesting career. I now began to specialise in hospitality and did another placement working as a housekeeper. During my year in Germany, I specialised in transport.'

When she graduated, Gwendael was immediately offered a job by the Concorde Hotel group and worked in central Paris as a housekeeper for seven months. Then came a position as assistant executive housekeeper at a resort hotel in the Lebanon. This was a very different type of hotel. 'I was responsible for the swimming pools and beach area as well as the public areas and bedrooms. I walked one and a half miles twice a day while doing my rounds.'

She moved to Cardiff two years ago, found a job in a local hotel; then came to the Hilton in April 2001.

What does Gwendael's day involve?

'It depends partly on which shift I am on, but if it is the day shift I would come in at about 9am. I check with my supervisors that everyone is in and that we are fully staffed, then open up the pantries containing the room attendants' trolleys – they each have their own with their own cleaning materials. Next, I check the night duty manager's log to see whether anything needs to be done in any of the rooms. There might be a faulty light or something wrong with the air conditioning for example. I always have coffee with the duty supervisor so that we can discuss any problems. What I do for the rest of the day varies but I always do "walkabouts" during the shift. These are very important. I will also check the following week's occupancy rate and match that with the number of staff needed, check stocks, order supplies, arrange for contractors to come and clean carpets, look at questionnaires completed by "mystery guests" or do some training.

'I usually have a brief feedback meeting with all the staff around midday. I spend a lot of time talking to staff. The room attendants are all female – many have children and they might need time off to cope with illness or child care problems. I also have to do disciplinary work from time to time and might need advice from the Human Resources Department on this.

'I have a budget to manage – for cleaning materials, supplies of toiletries to bedrooms, flowers for the public rooms (I employ a local florist), laundry, and repairs to any damage caused to furnishings. I might have to negotiate with a laundry that is imposing what I consider too high a price increase – or get quotes for replacing damaged fabric. I recently had a problem over a cigarette burn to a chair. The original material had been specially produced for us and the manufacturer would now have to do a special order involving a minimum amount of fabric. Very expensive!

'I usually leave about six or seven in the evening after a ten-hour day. But the time flies. I sometimes wonder where the day has gone! I also take a turn at being the duty manager, responsible for the entire hotel. I usually choose the shift that ends at 1am so that I can talk to the night cleaners and porters. I love the work. I enjoy working in all areas of the hotel and I like meeting guests. I want to make sure that my guests are as comfortable as they would be in their own homes.'

Hotel manager

A hotel manager's role is to ensure that the hotel is operating efficiently and profitably and to be responsible for every aspect of the running of a hotel – both day and night. Their duties cover everything from budgeting, forward planning, marketing and sales to staff recruitment and training. The work varies depending on the size of the hotel and the number of staff. In a small hotel there may be only one manager, while in large ones there is a management team headed by a general manager who has one or more deputy general managers and a team of specialist managers all reporting to him/her. The general manager is then concerned with strategy and increasing profit (and will have an operations manager to oversee the day-to-day running of the hotel). An important part of the work is developing new business and most managers stay in close touch with their local tourist boards who can inform them of any large events or conferences planned which would require bedrooms and meeting rooms. They also contact businesses and organisations, hoping to persuade them to use the hotel for their functions, and think of ideas for special events. (Where a sales or marketing manager is employed, some of this work would be done by him/her.) Most general managers hold several meetings every week with their departmental managers to discuss the current situation, special events profits and future plans – for several months or even one or two years ahead. (See individual management entries in this chapter for details of specialist management roles.)

Skills required

- Outgoing personality
- Leadership
- Communication skills
- Organisational ability
- Knowledge of the work of every department – accommodation, food and beverage operations, plus finance, marketing and personnel
- Languages are useful.

Entry routes

- Many managers now have degrees or diplomas, although it is still possible to be promoted from junior positions.
- Entry to management training schemes usually requires a degree, Higher National Diploma or membership of the Hotel, Catering and International Management Association.
- Successful experience in departmental management posts is also required. (Moving up through the food and beverage departments, as opposed to working front of house, is the most usual route.)

Career prospects

Hotel managers have several options. They could move to larger hotels, transfer to other jobs in their own hotel chain – like marketing or training – or they could move into other business areas.

CASE STUDY

Hotel General Manager, Mark Walker

Mark is the general manager of the 197-room Hilton Hotel in Cardiff. He says, 'My role is rather like that of an orchestra conductor – making sure that everyone is playing the right tune, and at the right time.'

A general manager has a team of senior managers to run different parts of the hotel. Other than keeping on top of what they are all doing and taking ultimate responsibility for running the establishment, he or she has a more strategic role. Mark says, 'My job is to keep business coming in and take it forward. At the end of the day, I am responsible for sales, profits and customer service. I have a key team: operations manager (responsible for the day-to-day running of the hotel), a revenue manager, human resources manager and financial controller. They in turn have their own teams of supervisors and staff.

'I hold a daily 30-minute senior team meeting, and then liaise at some point during the day with each of the senior managers. I sit in on and have some input to the weekly operations meeting which the operations manager holds with his managers. I chair the weekly sales meeting – and I spend a good deal of time in public relations work, keeping the hotel in the public eye. I try to get one article each week featuring the hotel by name in the local press. One success has been to establish a weekly column in one paper written by our chef. We are active in the community. One thing we are doing at the moment is a project by the senior managers who are doing a local variety of "Changing Rooms" for senior citizens. I am on the board of the University of Wales Institute, Cardiff (which runs several degree and diploma courses in hospitality) and on the board of Springboard Wales (the hospitality industry's careers organisation).

'Marketing the hotel is extremely important. I know in my head what our plans and targets are for up to six months ahead. I monitor closely what the two sales managers are doing and often accompany them on calls. I also take an active part myself. I attend at least two functions outside the hotel every week. Networking is very important when it comes to creating new business. I am always looking for new opportunities – to encourage organisations and businesses to come here for conferences and functions.

'But the job is not just about meetings and future plans. I walk around constantly, watching, looking, seeing how the staff are getting on, how guests are being served. (And if we do receive any letters of complaint, I ring the writer personally to apologise. I think touches like that are important.) I may even help out occasionally if there are staff shortages in any areas. Even senior managers have to be hands-on in this business. If we were under pressure, I would carry plates from the kitchen to the restaurant myself rather than see guests waiting for their food.'

What hours does he work?

'From about 8.15am until 7.30pm from Monday to Friday. I come in on Saturday mornings to clear the post, and in the evenings if necessary, and never work on Sundays. They are for the family. However, I stay much later on evenings when we have big events.'

Mark's career history

Mark did a Higher National Diploma course at Westminster College, a well-known catering college in London. Training in London, he says, was good because there was plenty of opportunity to get part-time work and experience in five-star hotels. On leaving Westminster, he became a management trainee with a small group of exclusive four- and five-star hotels and worked in three different hotels in two years. Next came jobs (with promotion) to operations manager in two privately owned hotels (including one where Gary Rhodes worked for him as chef) until he decided that he preferred the buzz of larger establishments and moved back to a large group. He worked as deputy manager in one before being headhunted and invited to open a new hotel of 95 rooms – 'good experience for a first general manager's position', then was headhunted again by the Stakis Group. Hilton bought Stakis – and he has been in Cardiff since September 2001.

Personnel and training manager

Personnel and training managers are responsible for the recruitment and training of staff and for their career development. In very large hotels the functions may be split and there will be different managers for personnel work and for training. The work is similar to that of personnel and training managers in all industries and includes preparing job descriptions, advertising for staff, interviewing, keeping personnel records, identifying training needs and arranging training programmes, appraising performance and developing personnel policy. Personnel and training managers may also be responsible for producing the hotel's health and safety policy, operating a pension scheme and providing a staff welfare service.

Skills required

- Communication
- Administrative and training skills
- Tact and diplomacy.

Entry routes

- Through a hotel's management training scheme.
- By obtaining personnel and training experience elsewhere.

Some managers have diplomas or degrees in hotel and catering subjects; others have business studies or personnel qualifications. Some may be members of the Chartered Institute of Personnel and Development.

Career prospects

Personnel managers have the option of moving to larger hospitality businesses or out of the area altogether and becoming human resources managers for other types of organisation.

Purser

A large passenger ship is like a floating hotel and all the kinds of staff who can be found in a hotel – chefs, waiters, cleaners, front-of-house staff, receptionists, etc – work within the ship's hotel services department. In some shipping companies, the term 'purser' is used to describe the hotel services general manager (a very senior post on a passenger ship), but the term more usually refers to a senior member of the hotel department who combines some of the functions of a front-of-house manager and food and beverage manager. The purser's department usually handles all the ship's accounts, administration and paperwork, orders supplies and allocates cabins. The purser is a ship's officer.

On passenger aircraft, the purser is responsible for cabin service and the work of all the cabin crew; on Eurostar trains, for the work of catering stewards and stewardesses.

Skills required
As for hotel manager.

Entry routes
Most pursers have had experience in one of the management jobs in a hotel. See hotel manager, food and beverage manager, etc.

Career prospects
Pursers could move between different sectors – hotels, shipping companies, airlines, etc.

CASE STUDY

Duty On-Board Services Manager Co-ordinator, Karen Willett

Karen works for Momentum Services, the company that supplies catering staff to work on Eurostar trains.

She left school with A-levels and completed the first year of a degree course in combined studies, then left. Why? 'It seems odd now but one of my subjects was French. It was going to involve a year's study abroad and I decided that I didn't want to do that. I did some temporary work in hotels and pubs for a while – then suddenly I found myself in France after all! I decided to improve my French and found a job as an au pair. From there I went to work in a hotel in Tignes, a ski resort. My French improved rapidly. I got a job in a hotel in Corsica for the summer season and went back to the hotel in Tignes for the winter. I was promoted there and became head waiter. It was then that I saw the advertisement for catering staff to work for Eurostar and decided to apply.'

She returned to London for the interview, where her French was tested – by a French person. 'I think I was quite a surprise,' she says. 'English people are on the whole very bad at languages. In fact English staff are in the minority in our on-board teams for that very reason.'

On-board catering staff receive a month's initial training. This begins with an introduction to both companies – Momentum and Eurostar, then covers basic first aid, safety (including tunnel evacuation procedures) and customer service for both First and Standard Class passengers. Practice is done in a mock-up train section where they learn to prepare meals in the galley, work behind the buffet counter, serve meals to passengers in First Class and provide a trolley service of drinks and snacks. They do one return journey to Paris or Brussels for familiarisation purposes and finally work on-board for three days with a 'buddy', a qualified crew member who helps them to do all the tasks in a real work situation and get up to speed. Finally, they are tested on everything they have learned during training, including French and mental arithmetic. (Customers may pay for purchases in pounds, euros or US dollars, so staff must be competent in handling and converting all three currencies.) If successful, they are assigned to a team.

Each team member does one return journey each day to Brussels, Lille or Paris and may have a stopover of up to five and a half hours before returning. They have to work shifts since trains run between 5am and midnight, but do return to base every day. If the tunnel was closed or service was disrupted for some other reason, they might have to stay in a hotel and are expected to carry overnight essentials on all journeys.

Karen worked as a stewardess for just over a year before being promoted to purser. What does that role involve?

'There are two pursers on each train, each responsible for on-board services in one half of the train. They have a crew of up to 12, depending on how full the train is. They are responsible for all customer service in their half and also for answering any questions from passengers. The purser is more than a senior steward. The role is wider and includes assessing staff performance – and recommending them for promotion to work in First Class (for which they receive a further week's training).'

The next step up the career ladder is to the position of Duty On-Board Services Manager (DOBS). There are nine DOBS in London, each managing a group of pursers and staff. They are expected to make around 12 journeys each month to assess staff working on board. Some assist with recruitment and selection or running the introductory training courses.

As DOBS Co-ordinator, Karen's job is very varied. She says 'I now manage all the London DOBS, spend a lot of time liaising between my own company and Eurostar and also do some recruitment and selection work. I am involved in training too. On training courses for First Class work. I act as a passenger. I now work mainly Monday to Friday but I still do about five journeys a month – and that includes weekends. Back in London I spend a lot of time in meetings with both Momentum and Eurostar staff. I check the quality of customer service constantly – which includes analysing customer satisfaction surveys or reports by "mystery shoppers" who have been on board. But anything can happen at any time and I have to think on my feet. I might get a call from a purser on the train, asking for advice on dealing with a problem that has just occurred or get the news that a train has been delayed. In that case, I have to work out how we are going to get our crew back to London. I have to think about the passengers too. We always keep our own staff with them in any problem situation. If, for instance, a Eurostar train broke down in Kent and passengers had to be transferred to the local train company's trains, our staff would travel back to London with them on that train.'

What does Karen like about working for Eurostar?

'The variety. Every day is different. You never know what it will bring. On the trains you might have to deal with illness or complaints or even nervous passengers. I have had to sit for the 20-minute journey through the tunnel with people who suddenly become frightened at the thought of being under the sea. I've worked on trains going to ski resorts where there is a real party atmosphere – and on ones full of excited children going to Disneyland Paris. I loved the passenger contact – and still have some, but I enjoy the responsibility I now have in this job. I have been very lucky. I joined a young company and have been able to progress quickly.'

Career note

The minimum requirements to work as a steward/stewardess are GCSE or equivalent in English and maths, previous experience in catering or customer care and a basic level of spoken French. Crew must be prepared to live within one hour's journey of their home station – in either Brussels, London or Paris.

Sales and marketing manager

Large hotels employ specialist managers whose job is to try to fill as many of the bedrooms as possible, ensure that function and conference suites are fully used and generally promote all services and facilities of the hotel. The work involves: market research to identify potential customers; devising events such as special interest weekends; and producing literature to market the hotel, including general leaflets, conference packs or information for the travel trade; advertising and promotional activities. Sales and marketing managers may also be involved in showing potential customers around the hotel and representing the hotel at trade fairs.

With hotel chains, the marketing strategy and pricing policy may be set by the head office. In independent hotels, the general manager may undertake all aspects of sales and marketing.

Skills required

- Knowledge of sales and marketing techniques
- Outgoing personality
- Persuasive ability
- Initiative
- Ability to establish good working relationships with a wide range of people
- Foreign language skills are useful.

Entry routes

- Through gaining experience in other areas of hotel management, for example, in the conference and banqueting area
- From a management training programme
- Through marketing experience gained outside the hotel and catering industry.

Many sales and marketing managers have HNDs or degrees either in hotel and catering management or in marketing.

Career prospects

There are opportunities to move to more highly paid jobs either in hotel and catering organisations or in other industries.

Chapter 4
PROFESSIONAL QUALIFICATIONS

Attending full-time courses is not the only way to obtain qualifications that will improve your career prospects. There is a range of qualifications that can be obtained by people who want to progress in their careers but are unable to take full-time courses or even to attend regular part-time courses because of the shifts that they work. As you will have seen in Chapter 2 – Training, it is possible to gain NVQs and SVQs while at college or on a training scheme. They can also be obtained in employment.

WHAT ARE NVQs AND SVQs?

National Vocational Qualifications are awarded in England and Wales; Scottish Vocational Qualifications in Scotland. They are work-related qualifications that demonstrate what someone is capable of doing – and are available at five levels, ranging from Level 1 designed for new entrants to a career right up to Level 5 which equates to higher degree level. Unlike more traditional qualifications, they are not gained by passing examinations but by being assessed at work by an approved assessor who has relevant training and experience in the particular industry. In the hotel and catering industry, NVQs and SVQs are available in all the major areas of food preparation and cookery, food and drink service, housekeeping and reception. Many are available up to Level 3; few beyond that.

People working towards NVQs/SVQs are required to record their achievements as they become capable of them and to present a portfolio of evidence as part of the assessment. This is normally done by keeping a log or work book and obtaining a signature from a supervisor or manager when an appropriate level of competence has been achieved in a particular task. Some hotel and catering employers have managers and supervisors who have trained to become assessors. Others use external assessors.

The Hospitality Training Foundation lists eight different NVQs/SVQs at Level 1 in hotel and catering work:

- Food and Drink Service
- Food Preparation and Cooking
- Guest Service
- Housekeeping
- Kitchen/Portering
- Porter Service
- Preparing and Serving Food
- Reception.

At Level 2, it lists ten:

- Bar Service
- Food and Drink Service
- Food Preparation and Cooking
- Food Processing and Cooking
- Hospitality Quick Service
- Hospitality Services
- Housekeeping
- Reception
- Residential Services
- Special Dietary Requirements.

A trainee chef, for example, working towards an NVQ Level 2 in Food Preparation and Cooking would be expected to demonstrate competence in preparing and cooking basic hot and cold dishes (including desserts, pasta, salads, sauces, soups, rice, and vegetarian dishes), assembling food, handling and storing food deliveries and cleaning food production areas and equipment.

Level 3 has ten NVQs/SVQs:

- Accommodation Supervision
- Drink Service Advanced Craft
- Food Preparation and Cooking
- Front Office Supervision
- Kitchen and Larder

- Kitchen Supervision
- Multi-Skilled Hospitality
- On-Licensed Premises Supervision
- Patisserie and Confectionery
- Restaurant Supervision.

At Level 4, there are two:

- Kitchen and Larder Specialist
- Patisserie and Confectionery Specialist.

OTHER PROFESSIONAL QUALIFICATIONS

The following organisations offer other professional qualifications.

The British Institute of Innkeeping (BII)

The BII is the national professional membership organisation for the licensed retail sector. It has 15,500 members, mostly individual licensees. It offers over 60,000 qualifications, ranging from National Licensee's and Scottish Licensee's Certificates (designed to give knowledge of the legal and social responsibilities involved in selling alcohol) to barpersons', door supervisors' and managers' certificates. The Institute also offers specialist courses in beer and wine knowledge. Training is usually completed through attendance at short courses at approved training centres.

The Hotel and Catering International Management Association (HCIMA)

The HCIMA is a professional association for people working in all branches of the hotel and catering industry. It provides various services for its members, such as social and business events, publications, advice on business planning and careers advice throughout their careers. It also awards two professional qualifications.

The HCIMA Professional Certificate is for supervisors working in the industry who wish to gain a qualification while remaining in employment. The certificate programme can be followed by part-time attendance at colleges throughout the UK. Someone able to attend college for one day a week would complete the programme in two years. Alternative methods are available. For example, a college might teach the course on two half days if that was more suitable for its local employers and students who cannot attend during the day might be able to find a college offering evening courses. Distance learning is another method – and is very suitable for people who are some distance from any suitable courses. In order to enrol on a certificate course, supervisors need to have an NVQ/SVQ Level 2 or equivalent qualification.

(The certificate course may also be taken on a one-year full-time basis.)

The HCIMA Professional Diploma is for people who are working in a position that gives them responsibilities in a department or section. They need in addition a qualification like a dual award vocational A-level (or equivalent qualifications like a national diploma – its predecessor). The diploma may also be studied through full-time, part-time or distance learning methods.

The Wine and Spirit Education Trust

Many wine waiters, pub managers/owners, restaurant managers and food and beverage managers obtain qualifications awarded by this organisation in order to improve their career prospects. There are three major qualifications:

- Intermediate Certificate in Wines, Spirits and other Alcoholic Beverages
- Advanced Certificate in Wines and Spirits
- Diploma in Wines and Spirits.

On these courses you would study the history of wine, wine making, wines from Europe and the New World, sparkling wines, liqueurs, spirits, beers, cider and legislation.

There is also a Spirits Course which does not at present lead to a formal qualification. Courses may be taken through evening classes or by short full-time courses. (The Intermediate Certificate, for example, would take eight two-hour evening sessions or three full days.) Each course leads to an examination.

Students who are successful in obtaining the diploma may go on to study for the prestigious Master of Wine qualification of the Institute of Masters of Wine. This is such a high level of qualification that there are only 236 members in the world – living in 16 different countries. The Institute's examination is held annually.

FURTHER INFORMATION

PUBLICATIONS

Caterer and Hotelkeeper magazine.

Hospitality Management. AGCAS.

Occupations. An annual careers guide . Department for Education and Skills (DfES).

UCAS handbook. A list of higher education courses.

Working in Hotels and Catering. DfES.

ADDRESSES

Information is available from the following organisations

British Institute of Innkeeping
Leisure Careers UK
Wessex House
80 Park Street
Camberley
Surrey GU15 3PT
Tel: 01276 684449
Website: www.bii.org

Hotel and Catering International Management Association
191 Trinity Road
London SW17 7HN
Tel: 020 8772 7400
Website: http://hcima.org.uk

The Institute of Masters of Wine
Five Kings House

1 Queen Street Place
London EC4R 1QS
Tel: 020 7236 4427

Springboard UK (The industry's own careers advisory service)
3 Denmark Street
London WC2H 8LP
Tel: 020 7497 8654
Website: www.springboarduk.org.uk

53–55 Kings Street
Glasgow G1 5RA
Tel: 0141 552 5554
Website: www.springboarduk.org.uk

47 Newport Road
Cardiff CF2 1AD
Tel: 029 2048 4899
Website: www.springboarduk.org.uk
(Contact the above national offices for addresses of regional offices)

Universities and Colleges Admissions Service (UCAS)
Rosehill
New Barn Lane
Cheltenham
Gloucestershire GL52 3LZ

The Wine and Spirit Education Trust
Five Kings House
1 Queen Street Place
London EC4R 1QS
Tel: 020 7246 1535
Website: www.wset.co.uk

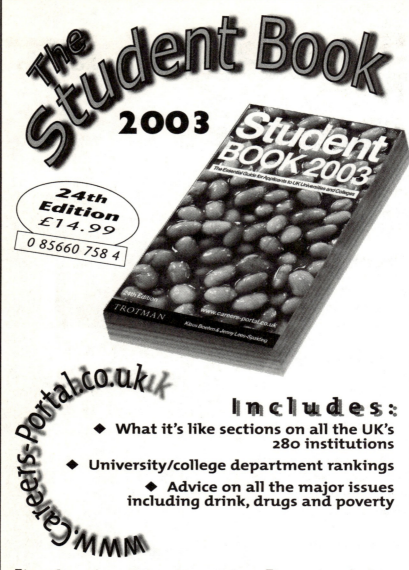

St Andrews RC